SIX ENEMIES OF FULFILLED DESTINY

SIX ENEMIES OF FULFILLED DESTINY
by
JOHN BURTON

Six Enemies of Fulfilled Destiny

Published by Revival Nation Publishing

ISBN 978-1-926625-16-4

Cover design by John Burton
www.johnburtondesign.com

Printed in the United States of America

Revival Nation Publishing
Ontario • CANADA

P.O. Box 30001
RPO Eastland Plaza
Sarnia, Ontario
N7T 0A7

www.RevivalNationPublishing.com
1-866-487-1361

To my children, Skylar, Parker, Jet and any not yet here. Refuse to look for the well-worn path but rather tear through every obstacle as you go where none have gone before. You will chart uncharted territories so your children can live well and launch out on their own journey from a firm foundation.

John and Amy Burton planted Revolution House of Prayer in Manitou Springs, Colorado in 2001. This ministry of intercession, warfare, and strategic Kingdom advance is the first piece of the puzzle in what will ultimately be a region-wide revival.

In 1991 John received a life-changing assignment from God to see an entire city set free. Over the years, God added to that vision and has since revealed that His dream is to see Manitou Springs transformed into an entire city that ministers to God 24 hours a day. That launched the Revolution team into a fresh season as a house of prayer, a house of worship and a house of dreams for the Pikes Peak region and way, way beyond!

John's ministry style could be described as wildly passionate, engaging, humorous and loaded with the flow and power of the Holy Spirit.

The prevailing theme of the ministry God has given John revolves around the topic of 'being with God.' Where God is, things happen. In His presence, the place where He is, is the fullness of joy. As we discover the wonderful mystery of walking in the Spirit, praying always and making aggressive strides in faith, life becomes incredible!

It truly is an experience in the invisible realm. As we tangibly experience God through deep and active prayer we are interacting 'in the Spirit.' As we walk by faith and understand how amazing a Holy Spirit driven life is, being a believer quickly becomes the greatest adventure on earth!

If you would like to invite John to speak at your church, conference, camp or other event, please visit www.johnburton.net.

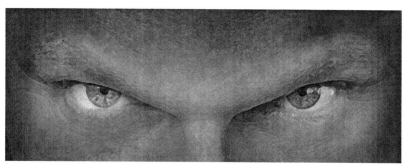

CONTENTS

INTRODUCTION

Currently you can find exactly 614,952 "How To..." books on a popular online bookseller. For less than twenty dollars you can learn "How to win friends and influence people," "How to change the world," "How to cheat at everything," "How to be an adult," "How to boil water," and even "How to read a book."

Planted in all of us at conception is a deep desire to fulfill our purpose on the Earth. Some are consumed by this persistent call to the point of fatigue, anxiety and burnout. The pressure to accomplish something, to climb the ladder of success or to be remembered after they die drives many to brokenness, drunkenness, divorce and even mental illness.

Others have tasted the bitterness of defeat and failure and have surrendered any thought of significance. Early in life they may have excitedly read, "How to change the world", but have long since put that book back to collect decades of dust on the bookshelf. Their preferred resources now read more like, "How to get a good night sleep" or "How to escape the pain of failure and rejection." Is it possible that you have been tempted to find a book like this?

I pray the book in your hands will help reignite the fire of passionate pursuit toward your fulfilled destiny.

I often ask God to ensure I don't end my time here on the Earth before I do all that I'm to do, know all that I am to know, experience all I'm to experience and impart all that I'm to impart. The mere thought of not completing my assignment is not an option. There is a deep yearning in all

> # Revelation will abound. Confidence will skyrocket. Passion will burn night and day.

of us to live an impossible life. To fall short of this goal means life will be lived well below the bar on mostly human power. Is this type of experience all there is?

No! There is a supernatural realm that we are to walk in every day of our lives. The more intent we are on ensuring our destiny is fulfilled and the goals of God in our lives are realized, the more the activity of God will increase in our lives. Our lives will be marked by testimony after testimony of supernatural activity, power and impartation. Revelation will abound. Confidence will skyrocket. Passion will burn night and day.

> Jeremiah 29:10-14 For thus says the Lord: After seventy years are completed at Babylon, I will visit you and perform My good word toward you, and cause you to return to this place. For I know the thoughts that I think toward you,

says the Lord, thoughts of peace and not of evil, to give you a future and a hope. Then you will call upon Me and go and pray to Me, and I will listen to you. And you will seek Me and find Me, when you search for Me with all your heart. I will be found by you, says the Lord, and I will bring you back from your captivity; I will gather you from all the nations and from all the places where I have driven you, says the Lord, and I will bring you to the place from which I cause you to be carried away captive.

You may be in a place of captivity now. If you are you can be comforted knowing that God is thinking about you. The passage in Jeremiah states that he has thoughts about you, thoughts of peace and not evil, thoughts to give you a future and a hope!

I don't know how you are wired, but I love to sit back and wonder exactly what God is thinking about me. What is in His mind right now regarding my future? What big plans and ideas has He considered for my life? That thought is enough to cause me to keep pressing on toward the goal!

As we proceed deeper into some of the specific enemies of fulfilled destiny, we'll gain clarity on the importance of being intentional in our pursuit. For now, let's just say that we should carefully consider the reality that the acquisition of God's promises and plans are largely dependent on our intentional participation. Many of God's promises are conditional. If this is the case, it would do us well to investigate just what those conditions are.

In the passage in Jeremiah it is clear that there is a significant season where God was withholding his visitation. After seventy years are completed God declared He would visit them and perform His Word. He then gives a word of encouragement: He has thoughts of peace, a future and a hope. However, if we simply sit back and relax at this point of the journey, we'll quickly grow weary and frustrated and even angry as it seems as if God has not done as He has promised. Where is the visitation? Where is peace? Where are my future and my hope?

Read on. We must, in faith and with great wisdom and zeal, pursue God. It's at God's appointed time, coupled with our vigilant participation, that we will step into a future of abundant life. The Scripture tells us that we must:

1. **Call.** One Hebrew interpretation uses the word 'accost.' The idea is that we fervently and aggressively call a meeting. We boldly approach the throne room. This call involves a fiery diligence from someone who simply cannot afford to be denied.

2. **Pray.** After the meeting with God commences as a result of our continual call, we pray. We intercede and make supplication. It's an engaging process of two-way communication as opposed to a five-minute recitation of a list of requests. We allow the Holy Spirit to pray through us; we groan and let the deep part of our spirit commune intimately with the Living God.

3. **Search with our whole heart.** Another way to say it is to frequently and diligently worship God. So our call led us to meet with God. Our intercession moved the heart of God and our continual worship places the focus on God instead of our own situation.

4. **Move.** Then, God will gather and bring us to a new place. It's the journey from the desert into the Promised Land. It can come quickly as we agree with God and are willing to face some giants. Or, we can wait forty years, or even die in the wilderness. Our inheritance, our fulfilled destiny, includes extreme battles, risk and

a reliance on God unlike any time in our previous lives. Few make it to this point.

So, as we embark on this thrilling and challenging journey of realizing a fulfilled destiny, let's pray.

Living God, beautiful Savior, I love you. I hunger for more of You– Your love, Your joy, Your activity in my life. I pray You would reveal Yourself as You are, in all Your beauty and splendor and power. I commit to going deeper every day. God, I want to do everything I have been called to do. I want to do this out of a fiery heart of love, joy, vision and determination. Thank You for being who You are in my life.

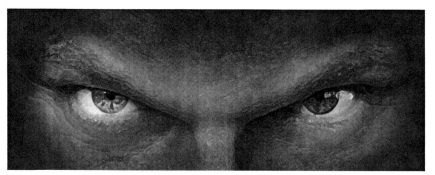

HEARING GOD

If you are familiar with my ministry or have read some of my other books, you will know that a core part of my heart is focused on the importance of prophecy and hearing God clearly, continually. God is a Person and He loves to dialogue. There is much to be said, instructions to be given, thoughts to be shared and truths to be imparted. Simply, God designed us to be able to hear His voice.

If our desire is to fulfill the destiny God has assigned to us, we must become experts at seeing what God sees– peering into His invisible realm, seeing in the Spirit, hearing in the Spirit and receiving constant data from that dimension! If we don't learn how to do this, we are in great danger of spiritual death!

If we can't see and hear, we become greatly dependent on the latest and greatest idea. Instead of pushing ahead into our unique calling with precise instructions from God Himself, we have no choice but to mimic and repeat what others have already accomplished.

We glean as much as we can from the latest book or conference, and instead of using such materials to enrich our lives, we find ourselves with little or no personal vision and in turn attempt to do what has already been done, usually with miserable results. Yes, we can and should learn a lot from many other people that God puts into our lives, but that knowledge and wisdom should be used to undergird our attempts to accomplish God's very personal and humanly impossible mission. God wants us to go where no man has gone before!

> Life is correspondence with environment. A child is born with five senses and various bodily organs, and each corresponds with something in his environment: the eye sees sights, the ear hears sounds, the lungs breathe air, and so on. While I can correspond with my environment, I have life, but if something happened to me which prevented me from corresponding with my environment then I should be dead; death is a failure of correspondence.- Rees Howells

What a powerful statement! Death is a failure of correspondence. This is what I mean when I say that unless we hear the voice of God, we are in danger of spiritual death. We must correspond with God in order to live.

God wants us to go where no man has gone before!

Take a moment and read a passage from my book, Revelation Driven Prayer:

Listen. Can you hear His voice? What's He saying?

Those questions have probably frustrated more people through the ages than we could fathom. Books have been written about unanswered prayer. The walls of pastors' and counselors' offices have soaked up countless quotes like, "I don't hear God," "God doesn't talk to me," "I have no idea what I'm supposed to do." And then, like clockwork, the question is asked to the counselor, "What do YOU think I should do?"

After all, to ask that question of someone we can see, and someone who can hear us, not to mention someone who will instantly talk back– audibly, so we can hear– seems to make a lot of sense. Certainly that person has the answers we're looking for, right? Well, sometimes yes, sometimes no.

In fact, if we are to fulfill our ministry, and if we are to move into uncharted territories, the majority of our direction will simply have to come directly from God himself. Others have not been where we are going!

1 Cor 2:5 (NKJV) ... your faith should not be in the wisdom of men but in the power of God.

If, throughout the Bible, God causes men and women to do things that defy human logic, why do we resort to common sense when making decisions in our lives? If God told Gideon to secure only 1% of his army to go into battle, which obviously defies solidly time-tested military wisdom, why don't we consider that God may also cause us to advance in our lives via untraditional and even bizarre means?

Job 11:7 (NIV) "Can you fathom the mysteries of God? Can you probe the limits of the Almighty?"

Mysteries! God has an impossible job for us to accomplish, and it is going to take creative ideas to fulfill our mission.

If we cannot hear God, how can we confidently make decisions? On the contrary, if we do hear God, we will have the boldness and confidence to move ahead regardless of how foolish it may seem. We trust that God is much smarter, wiser and more powerful than our friends, our pastor, our counselors and ourselves.

Romans 11:33 (NIV) Oh, the depth of the riches of the wisdom and knowledge of God!

1 Cor 1:25 (NKJV) Because the foolishness of God is wiser than men, and the weakness of God is stronger than men.

So, if we are operating in the Rhema wisdom of God, and that wisdom blows away the wisdom of man, that means many times God will be calling us to do something very different than what common sense or human wisdom would suggest. The advice in the counselor's office just won't cut it sometimes!

Is this to say we should never seek counsel? Of course not! The Bible states clearly that there is safety in a multitude of counselors. Absolutely! However, to default to human logic in neglect of the present voice of God Himself is a very average, not to say dangerous way to live.

God has a specific plan mapped out for us, and we must do an excellent job of receiving His instructions so our destiny can be sure!

Consider the following questions:

- From where are you receiving your instructions?
- How do you know what to plan for, how to pray, what to declare, what to do in any given day of your life?

• Is what you are doing right now a purposed activity to ensure your destiny comes to pass, or is it in response to the demands of survival?

> Be careful. A survivalist's mind-set will commonly cause us to move in the opposite direction of destiny!

Be careful. A survivalist's mind-set will commonly cause us to move in the opposite direction of destiny! If we are to fulfill our destiny, it will require precision, blood, sweat, tears, passion, focus and fire in our eyes as we stare death in the face!

The fulfillment of our destiny will result in many people in heaven. The failure of fulfilling our destiny will result in many people living in hell forever.

Nobody's destiny is hell, yet most people will end up there!

Let's look at that passage in Jeremiah again. We'll back up and start at the beginning of the chapter.

Notice the importance God places on hearing His instructions clearly:

Thus says the Lord of hosts, the God of Israel, to all who were carried away captive, whom I have caused to be carried away from Jerusalem to Babylon: Build houses and dwell in them; plant gardens and eat their fruit. Take wives and beget sons and daughters; and take wives for your sons and give your daughters to husbands, so that they may bear sons and daughters--that you may be increased there, and not diminished. And seek the peace of the city where I have caused you to be carried away captive, and pray to the Lord for it; for in its peace you will have peace. For thus says the

Lord of hosts, the God of Israel: Do not let your prophets and your diviners who are in your midst deceive you, nor listen to your dreams which you cause to be dreamed. For they prophesy falsely to you in My name; I have not sent them, says the Lord. For thus says the Lord: After seventy years are completed at Babylon, I will visit you and perform My good word toward you, and cause you to return to this place. For I know the thoughts that I think toward you, says the Lord, thoughts of peace and not of evil, to give you a future and a hope. Then you will call upon Me and go and pray to Me, and I will listen to you. And you will seek Me and find Me, when you search for Me with all your heart. I will be found by you, says the Lord, and I will bring you back from your captivity; I will gather you from all the nations and from all the places where I have driven you, says the Lord, and I will bring you to the place from which I cause you to be carried away captive.- Jeremiah 29:4-14 (NKJV)

Okay, let's break it down. God acknowledges the problem of captivity and is now giving instructions on how to experience deliverance.

In the first part of the chapter we see God directing them to do some things: build houses, plant gardens, get married and seek peace for the city of their captivity. At the risk of over simplifying the process I want to draw your attention to something. They had to hear God in order to know to begin working on these important tasks. Here they were in terribly devastating circumstances and God is requiring them to hear His voice and to respond accordingly.

I'll say this very clearly. We must not allow ourselves to embrace the lie that we are too bound up, too immature or too devastated to hear God's voice. Our very life and the lives of our succeeding generations are at great risk. The process out of captivity and into our destiny begins at the voice of God.

Now, God understands the trying circumstances of having to hear from Heaven while distraught and weak. God knows this can be challenging. We see Him give a clear warning not to let false prophets or diviners deceive them.

I have a strong opinion that we must honor God's appointed authority, and that we are called to respond to His Word as delivered through those who are watching out for our souls. The office of prophet is a critical one. That being said, we will be held responsible for how we respond to prophetic directives. If it's from God and we don't comply, we'll be held accountable. Conversely if we allow those who are attempting to lead from a human or even demonic platform to sway us away from obeying God's Word, we'll suffer the consequences.

My book *Covens in the Church* deals with this critical issue of submission to authority in much more detail. It would do the Church well to gain insight on how to be appropriately positioned and responsive within God's ordained governmental structure.

So, I pray I'm clearly communicating the serious responsibility we have in regard to receiving God's directions for our lives. Before we even begin talking about the enemies of fulfilled destiny, we have to agree on the extreme nature of our calling and the seriousness of our role in the process.

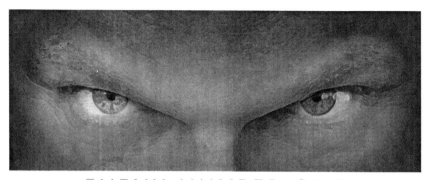

ENEMY NUMBER ONE
COMMON SENSE

Let's begin the investigation of this first enemy of fulfilled destiny by looking at a portion of my book *Revelation Driven Prayer*.

> Prov 3:5-7 (NKJV) Trust in the LORD with all your heart, And lean not on your own understanding; In all your ways acknowledge Him, And He shall direct your paths. Do not be wise in your own eyes;

> The verse actually tells us to basically resist our own understanding, to put little confidence in it. When I find myself saying, "I just don't understand," I get excited! This verse is a perfect verse for this book. It's the epitome of uncommon sense. Our own understanding, whether making decisions or developing strategies, can lead us astray. It can lead us into the predictable. It can be boring!

If we tend to make decisions based upon human wisdom and on proven strategies, then we limit God in ways beyond explanation. In essence, when we add prayer to that mind-set, we are asking God to bless our common plans instead of being available to bless God's uncommon plans!

The key to making uncommon-sense decisions is our prayer life. If we are praying continually, without ceasing, then we will hear God easily. We will capture His heart. We will know His desires. The sheep hear His voice.

John 10:3-4 (NKJV) "To him the doorkeeper opens, and the sheep hear his voice; and he calls his own sheep by name and leads them out. And when he brings out his own sheep, he goes before them; and the sheep follow him, for they know his voice."

All throughout Scripture we encounter decisions that defy human wisdom. David refused to wear the appropriate armor. Gideon took 1% of his potential army with him. Jesus put mud in somebody's eyes. In fact, the uncommon surpasses the common with incredible regularity.

If we can pay the price to continually pray, we'll continually hear God's voice. Our life will become radically different as we make decisions that defy human logic, that cause eyebrows to rise, and that will result in miraculous ending after miraculous ending!

Job 37:5 (NIV) God's voice thunders in marvelous ways; he does great things beyond our understanding.

Prayer is one of the most wonderful and essential activities for believers. One of my greatest joys is when I can help someone move beyond a petition–driven prayer life into a revelation–driven prayer life. When we pray what's on our heart ahead of what's on God's heart, we are greatly limited in our advance. As mentioned previously, we can become survival–minded instead of aggressively advancing into uncharted and threatening territory.

God has challenged me to embrace a new "prayeradigm," a new way of thinking in regard to my prayer life. Consider this. God in His wisdom has an agenda for us to follow when we're in prayer, or when we're communing in Him. This agenda includes many activities including intercession for cities, worship, declaring the Word of God, prophetic revelation, praying in tongues, etc. It's when I find myself aligned with this Holy Spirit–given agenda that I'm most refreshed, invigorated and confident in God's activity in my life. It takes discipline to avoid praying for anything not on the agenda. As I find myself praying "amiss," out of God's Holy Spirit–orchestrated flow, I grow weary. My well intentioned prayers birthed out of common sense actually cause me to retard my advance.

> My well intentioned prayers birthed out of common sense actually cause me to retard my advance.

Common sense, whether in prayer or in strategically advancing in ministry or in making daily decisions, can quickly impede and significantly limit our advance. We close ourselves in to what we can see with our eyes instead of learning to walk with our eyes shut and our spirit hot.

I have learned to love the part of Proverbs Chapter 3 that tells us not to lean on our own understanding. That single verse has brought adventure and opened huge new realms of possibility to my prayer life.

When something is on my heart or on my mind, I can be enticed to pray for a single obvious conclusion that is rooted in my own common sense. God taught me this lesson in part when I found myself praying with passion and faith (or so I thought) for a financial miracle.

As I usually do, I was pacing around the prayer room contending for a move of God. I was declaring with fervency a financial miracle that would result in certain bills being paid and other responsibilities being met.

My common sense gave me tunnel vision as I prayed for specific outcomes. In the midst of it all the Lord bellowed out to me, "Stop praying, John. Your prayer is doing damage."

What? If I didn't watch it, I could have been hurt or offended. After all, I was really praying with zeal. I'll never forget what God spoke to me. "John, what does My Word say about your needs being met?"

Oh. Of course. God's Word communicates clearly that all of my needs shall be met according to His riches in glory. God told me that since I didn't truly believe that, I found myself striking a pose of faith as I prayed fervently while I was actually filled with doubt. My doubt caused my prayer to be that much more zealous. The very fact that I was asking for my needs to be met revealed my doubt and mistrust of God in that area. By opening my mouth and releasing those prayers I was actually releasing doubt. Death. My "prayer" was doing more damage than good.

God took me on a journey of faith that opened up realms of wonder in the area of financial breakthrough. As I released my human common sense and allowed the wisdom and revelation of the Living God to be made manifest in me, I was taken in radically different directions than I would have ever considered in my own understanding.

Let's take just a moment for a disclaimer. You may be wondering if it's ever appropriate to use our common sense. It absolutely is. There are most definitely practical realities that we must understand. We can and should certainly learn from the trials of others and we can use our five senses to gain insight into any given situation. However, to default to common sense is a very average and even dangerous way to live. There are simply exponentially more Holy Spirit–driven options and directions and realities out there for us to discover. We don't want to cut short that wonderful and necessary journey.

It's All About Vision

The first part of this book discusses the importance of being able to hear God on a consistent basis. The reason we had to spend time on that topic is largely because of the need to receive clear vision.

> Where there is no revelation, the people cast off restraint; But happy is he who keeps the law. Proverbs 29:18 (NKJV)

You have probably read this verse many times, yet it's compelling enough to revisit. It could be interpreted this way:

> Where there is no prophetic revelation, oracles or dreams, entire groups of people perish and are unrestrained. But

happy is he who hears God's word and keeps it.

If we don't have revelation, a God-breathed vision, many others will suffer, in addition to ourselves.

However, as we receive God's prophetic revelation in our lives, both for our current season of life and also for our broader life mission, we will remain restrained and trained on that call. Many will be saved. We are happy, blessed, filled and invigorated when God's Word infuses us on a continual basis.

So, as we in the earlier part of our Christian walk discover our broad yet precise life mission, as we gain that burning vision that will not go out, we'll nearly immediately realize that tried and true methods that rely on common sense and human wisdom won't even get us out the door.

Many wonderful Christian people find themselves giving up the race at this early stage due to an inability to hear God's voice and, in effect, do not receive His vision for their lives. A lack of hearing causes many to believe that God has no significant calling for them beyond the obvious, or beyond common sense. So, we have many people who simply assume they are to default to being a good parent and a supportive spouse and possibly one who attends to the poor in the soup kitchen on occasion or who will teach a Sunday School class.

Are these important ministries? Yes. Yes, they are. Without question. But, to stop there and proceed no further because of a lack of reportable vision will result in disappointment, frustration and even burn out. You see, there is a difference between someone who works with children as a good-hearted servant and someone whose veins burn with the fire of Holy Spirit–birthed vision for ministering to the children of the world. They dream about it, have received specific outlines from God Himself for teaching and weep with great emotion when they even think of a child who doesn't know God. That's a big difference.

How did that children's minister get to that place of zeal? He heard God. How will He see such an all-consuming and humanly impossible vision fulfilled? By gaining Holy Spirit–seeded insight day after day, month after month and year after year. Methods of old won't work. Conferences may help, but will fall miserably short as effective suppliers of fresh and uniquely personal revelation for a uniquely personal task.

There's a commonly misquoted popular phrase:

Be a jack of all trades and master of none.

Many who find themselves without a unique and personal calling can become dangerously affirmed in their lack. Ben Franklin actually said something much more profound:

"Jack of all trades, master of One. A cultured person is one who knows Something about everything Everything about something."- Benjamin Franklin

Friend, we have no option but to find that something that God has for us to become an expert in. God being transcendent, omniscient, the Creator of atoms and galaxies, emotions and all truth is the One who is calling us into a wildly supernatural and invisible realm. This indescribable God has mysteries to reveal to us. There are places to go where no man has gone. In order to move from our current human experience (Point A) to this dimension of mystery, fire and fresh revelation of the living God, it requires that we move according to the voice of the Spirit. We must know that voice. We must trust that voice. We must lean not on our own understanding.

> "Can you fathom the mysteries of God? Can you probe the limits of the Almighty?" Job 11:7 (NIV)

So, as an example, according to that great quote by Benjamin Franklin, we should be familiar with children's ministry, the soup kitchen, teaching Sunday School, and witnessing to the lost. In addition to all of that (and much more) there is a very personal, unique and precise supernatural and humanly impossible vision and life mission that God has for each of us. We are called to be experts in this and to pave the way for many to follow after us. This will require that we lean not on our own understanding.

We must– let me say it again. We MUST diligently press in and go deep on a continual, daily basis. We won't discover the intricacies of our assignment unless we discover the intricacies of the Giver of the assignment. It won't happen without our persistent involvement as voluntary lovers of Jesus. Just today I heard Mike Bickle from the International House of Prayer in Kansas City say something that is amazingly simple yet profound:

You can't go deep in God on the run.

I pray that the more you understand the depth and magnitude of your calling, whether it's been fully revealed to you at this point or not, the more it will require a continually deeper revelation of the mysteries and glories of God. To truly go deep in God requires that we spend seemingly insane time with Him. We must learn to hear his voice in prayer. The wonder of this is that it's the most awe-inspiring and wholly fulfilling way we could spend our time!

If we rely on common sense and human wisdom for our lives, we'll quickly discount deep prayer as a necessary part of our lives.

> **If we rely on common sense and human wisdom for our lives, we'll quickly discount deep prayer as a necessary part of our lives.**

However, on the contrary, the moment we receive even a slight portion of the grand vision God has for us we'll find ourselves broken, weak and desperate for an infusion from on High day after day, month after month and year after year.

In his book, "Prayer", Hans Urs von Balthasar says:

> All of a sudden we just know: prayer is a conversation in which God's word has the initiative and we, for the moment, can be nothing more than listeners. The essential thing is for us to hear God's word and discover from it how to respond to him. His word is the truth, opened up to us.

"This is My beloved Son, in whom I am well pleased. Hear Him!" Matthew 17:5 (NKJV)

"The word is near you, in your mouth and in your heart." Romans 10:8 (NKJV)

Hans goes on to say,

> Man was created to be a hearer of the word, and it is in responding to the word that he attains his true dignity. His innermost constitution has been designed for dialogue.

When life demands action on our part, the voice of God becomes a non–negotiable necessity on a moment-by-moment basis for the one who doesn't default to human common sense. A life of fervent prayer is their sustenance. Obstacles such as the cares of life that Jesus warned about are violently demolished. However, for the one who is comfortable or settled with the mundane and predictable yet greatly ineffective method of survival via human wisdom first and foremost, the discipline of training our ear to hear our Lord's voice becomes largely unnecessary. It's only when those efforts fail that a cry to Heaven is heard. This paradigm is evidenced in a variety of ways, including empty prayer rooms, stale strategies, vanilla dreams and little fire to live a transformed and transforming life.

Man was created to be a hearer of the Word of God. That is a deeply powerful truth. If this is a primary purpose of our creation, if we were given life by the breath of God and we are called to continually receive the fresh breath of His Word, it makes sense that our entire lives, our decisions and directions as we navigate life, should be in direct response to that breath. We move as God moves. We do as God does. We say what God says. We breathe the fire of God that's stimulated in us every day. We change atmospheres not through human might but through the invisible force that is translating the life of God in us continually day and night.

Get excited when you remember the verse that instructs us to not lean on our own understanding. This means instead of expecting the outcome based on a mortal and limited human, we can explode those expectations a million times a million times! Get ready to live a life of great surprises, impossibilities and miracles. Yes, be prepared to be sharpened, challenged, broken and called into some of the most trying and lonely times of your life. Allow God to wreck you and flow through you in ways that very few have allowed Him to do over the last several thousand years of human history.

Come, Holy Spirit. Come as You are. Do what You want. In me. Through me. Today.

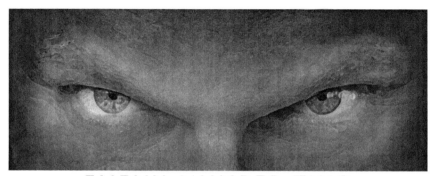

ENEMY NUMBER TWO
FELT NEEDS

Isaiah 11:1-3 (NKJV) There shall come forth a Rod from the stem of Jesse, And a Branch shall grow out of his roots. The Spirit of the LORD shall rest upon Him, The Spirit of wisdom and understanding, The Spirit of counsel and might, The Spirit of knowledge and of the fear of the LORD. His delight is in the fear of the LORD, And He shall not judge by the sight of His eyes, Nor decide by the hearing of His ears ...

Stop for just a moment and appreciate the weight of this passage. The reference is to Jesus, the Rod and the Branch- Almighty God. This is one of my favorite passages to pray over myself on a regular basis. The Spirit of the Lord in seven different manifestations would soon rest on Jesus as the Father knew that his life on the earth would demand these helps.

The same is true for you and me. Since we're fighting an invisible enemy and are pursuing an invisible fulfilled destiny, we should understand early in the process that our methods of navigation must be supernaturally charged. The compass of felt needs will lead us astray time and again while the compass of the Seven Spirits of the Lord will cause us to go where man power could never take us.

There is a Spirit of wisdom that will defy human wisdom.

Keep in mind that Jesus Himself would require this special and precious gift, a divinely tuned compass, in order for His terrible yet necessary and earthshaking destiny to be realized. If we are also called to carry our crosses and if we are given literally impossible mandates to steward to completion, we must refuse to default to the demand and seemingly logical reasoning of our felt needs and lay those thoughts before the Lord and seek a higher revelation.

There is a Spirit of wisdom that will defy human wisdom. There is a Spirit of understanding that will be necessary as we take steps into the unknown. These plus counsel, might, knowledge and the fear of the Lord will, when embraced as our supreme source of guidance, result in stunningly effective movement. We'll soberly and passionately, with Holy Spirit–given divine preparation, venture into the place of miracles, the impossible, the fearsome and new realms of authority, freedom and fulfillment.

Due to the impossible and urgent nature of our end-time callings, we have no option but to deal with the threat of being misguided by what is artificially urgent and humanly demanding, very tangible felt needs, with speed and without mercy. Those demands will hit us hard many times a day if we don't discover the strength of the fasted lifestyle. We must resist the force of felt needs and succumb to the call of the Lord. That call must be heard in the place of intimacy and zealous prayer on a moment-by-moment basis. It must be responded to even when our felt needs scream, our flesh squirms and our logic threatens to mock the wisdom of the Spirit of God.

> And my God shall supply all your need according to His riches in glory by Christ Jesus. Philippians 4:19 (NKJV)

This verse is referenced often when teaching on faith. It should be, as it is calling us into a dimension of life that is fueled by God Himself. God desires us to live on that edge without a Plan B. Notice that the verse relays a promise that our need shall be met or supplied according to something. Of course, we can easily see that our needs are met according to His riches in glory by Christ Jesus. Let's break it down a little further.

Many wonder why this verse doesn't work for them. They can't understand why they struggle. There are many directions we could go with this study, but for the sake of our topic let's investigate just one. Is it possible that often we misdiagnose our true need? In order to live a miraculous and fulfilled life where needs are met time and again, we must analyze our need. What is our calling? What are our goals? What is our mandate? What do we need to properly steward all of that? As we get serious about this, we'll quickly find ourselves re categorizing needs into other columns on the spreadsheet of our life. We will see that former needs have been re tagged as desires, obstacles, focuses of our old life, good ideas or selfish ambition. For example, our flesh will start to demand food after a missed meal. The felt need that hunger reveals can be quite demanding, but is called into submission during times of fasting. Desire can be very jealous of need. I once preached a sermon that focused on bringing light to the sneaky and selfish jealousy that desire has. Desire wants the attention that true need gets. It demands fulfillment.

The way we handle desire and need will determine the amount of joy we experience on a daily basis and the amount of victory as we pursue an accomplished life mission. When we realize that what we once thought were needs are actually not, we will find ourselves refreshed and energized to press toward the goal. The demands will fall away. We'll embrace God's revealed needs for our lives and our desires will become ordered and sanctified.

God knows how demanding true needs are, which is why He determined to ensure that all of our needs are met. If we can move from expending a majority of our energy on ensuring needs are met ourselves to taking a breath and understanding that every legitimate need is guaranteed to be met, we'll become quite successful and full of life.

So, if we can truly identify what a legitimate need is, and then understand that God will supply according to His riches in glory, we can get to work on ensuring our destiny is fulfilled. It becomes a wonderful way to live when we watch true needs met by God in fresh and supernatural ways. He's not meeting needs according to our presumed blueprints. That would be too predictable. God surprises us time and again as he dips into his mysterious resources and pours out into us.

So, according to God's riches, via the Seven Spirits of God we will live a wild, supernatural and victorious life.

I'd encourage you to sit down with a notebook and categorize the issues of your daily life into three columns: Needs, Desires and Distractions.

First, only focus on the left column. Ask God to reveal to you everything in your life that has mandated the attention of a need. In this first exercise you will list it all regardless of if it's a true need or a felt need. We'll separate them out later.

Example:

NEEDS	DESIRES	DISTRACTIONS
$500 more a month		
affirmation		
more friends		
time to relax		
a vacation		
food		
shelter		
a better job		
to be loved		
support my family		

Now, pray. Ask the Holy Spirit to reveal to you how the cares of life may have weighed you down. What felt needs have been exposed? Don't worry about putting down obvious desires at this point. The goal is to re categorize desires or distractions that have masqueraded as a need.

Duplicate your spreadsheet with the same three columns. Now, let's start moving some thieves of our energy and faith into their appropriate place.

NEEDS	DESIRES	DISTRACTIONS
money to pay bills		
→	affirmation	
→	more friends?	more friends?
time to relax		
→	a vacation	
food		
shelter		
→	a better job?	a better job?
to be loved		
support my family		

Does the load feel a bit lighter? If not, remember that when you have as pure an understanding as possible of true needs, your faith will be stirred up as you watch God meet those needs. Your energy won't be spent on meeting the demands of felt needs anymore. Your desires will take second place and will thus be less weighty and demanding on you.

The next step will take some time as you spend time in extended prayer. Ask God to fill in the rest of the blanks. Your list will probably be much longer than the one above. Let God reveal to you some additional needs that you may not have even been able to address due to everything else that was weighing you down. Your faith will again increase as God reveals just how he has met these newly revealed needs.

Then, we know that God loves to give us the desires of our heart. It's a wonderful thing when desires are properly categorized as such. We can then dream and become excitedly expectant as these desires stir in our hearts. When desires masquerade as needs, they are no fun at all to deal with. But, when we have pure, God-given desire burning inside of us night and day, we can dream and smile and rejoice like children!

Lastly, let God sort out what are actually distractions. Is the pursuit of a better job a desire, or is that want a distraction? Is it possible God may have you on assignment in your current workplace? If so, this revelation will result in a fresh dose of vision and energy.

> Now it happened as they went that He entered a certain village; and a certain woman named Martha welcomed Him into her house. And she had a sister called Mary, who also sat at Jesus' feet and heard His word. But Martha was distracted with much serving, and she approached Him and said, "Lord, do You not care that my sister has left me to serve alone? Therefore tell her to help me." And Jesus answered and said to her, "Martha, Martha, you are worried and troubled about many things. "But one thing is needed, and Mary has chosen that good part, which will not be taken away from her." Luke 10:38-42 (NKJV)

God is calling all of us away from a life of being worried and troubled. Martha was distracted with much serving, much activity. She felt that there were certain needs that demanded her attention, but Jesus revealed that she was overly troubled. Martha didn't effectively receive the necessary wisdom and revelation to sort out the various demands of the moment. Mary did have that revelation, and that is a moment at the feet of Jesus that she'll never forget. Jesus revealed that Martha was worried. I believe it would be fair to say that a high majority of Christians live their lives filled with worry most days.

> As we focus our energy on desire, we will live quite a life. Desire is one of the most powerful forces in the universe.

Worry is atheism. It says, "There is no God." It pulls control out of God's hands and into our own. When we realize we don't have what it takes to make ends meet, anxiety floods in. When the left column is overloaded, when there are false needs weighing us down, legitimate needs become way too much for us to handle. Fear and anxiety become our immediate and consistent response.

God's purpose for need is to teach us how to dream. If our needs aren't given to him, God knows that desires also won't be given to him. If we don't have faith to see needs met, which take the least faith of any part of our life, we won't have the faith to stimulate desires and release them into God's hands. We won't have faith to step out into the impossible desires God wants to give us.

Desires like:
1. Winning many to Jesus
2. Taking a city for God
3. Millions of dollars flowing through us into the ministry
4. Prophesying, dreaming dreams and having visions
5. Healing the sick
6. Growing in righteousness
7. Impacting nations

8.   Fulfilling our ministry!

God knows that abundant life doesn't come from crises after crises in regard to straining to have our needs met. Abundant life comes when we are in His presence, we don't think about our need and we become dreamers with deep and intoxicating God–given desires!

> The poor shall eat and be satisfied; Those who seek Him will praise the LORD. Let your heart live forever!
> Psalms 22:26 (NKJV)

The enemy wants us to fear and doubt that our needs will be met. He doesn't want us to be with God, to dream, to move into a place of life–changing desire! God knew needs were demanding; this is why He guaranteed 100% that they would be met!

> And my God shall supply all your need according to His riches in glory by Christ Jesus. Philippians 4:19 (NKJV)

When we identify true needs and embrace this Scripture as a settled issue, we will be launched into the dimension we were designed to thrive in, the dimension of God–birthed desire!

So, as we effectively deal with the issue of what is and what is not need we'll find ourselves very excited about life. We'll discover that to need is actually a good experience! Why? Because the needs are met! Met needs cause us to feel great!

As we focus our energy on desire, we will live quite a life. Desire is one of the most powerful forces in the universe. Need has the potential of holding someone back, yet desire has the potential of changing the world!

As we grow in faith by witnessing God take care of our every need, we can much more easily believe for God–birthed desires to come to pass.

"Well God, I've seen you pay the bills and you healed my wife and you delivered us from depression. My faith is strong. Let's go, God! Stir the impossible dream in my life! I'm ready and expectant! You've done it my life. Let's take it to a whole new level!"

The enemy is terrified of such a position. He understands all too well the power of holy desire. The power of the Holy Spirit can't be stopped when it's flowing through an excited, radical and agreed human vessel.

He knows that pure desire is fulfilling and invigorating even before it's fulfilled! Just as a bride is driven and full of joy and life in the weeks prior to the wedding, Satan knows that if we, as the bride of Christ, discover the awesome fulfillment of desire as we prepare for that great wedding day, the Church will be an unstoppable force! A holy people not weighed down by the cares of life– strike one– and who are full of joy at the mere thought of their Lover returning– strike two– and that this balance will result in the hastened return of the King– strike three! Satan loses! Do you see the power of holy desire?

In one last attempt to drive home the point of the importance of effectively categorizing needs, desires and distractions, I'll conclude with this.

Need demands attention. Desire, on the other hand, does not. That's the important difference between the two! So, the enemy will do whatever he can to put a mask on desire. He wants it to masquerade as a need.

"Look, I'm a need! I'm a need! Feed me! Feed me! Now! You won't be happy until you feed me! You won't be fulfilled until you worship me!"

The moment we lose focus of the dividing line between need and desire, the enemy will get a foothold. How can we know when desire has put on the mask? When we aren't fully joyful prior to desire being fulfilled. When it places a weight on us that seemingly will only be lifted if the desire is fulfilled. If dreaming about the fulfillment of the desire brings depression or frustration instead of excitement, it's a signal of a problem.

This is a vital lesson to be learned. The moment desire puts on the mask of need, we are saying that God isn't enough! That desire, even if God–birthed, becomes an idol. It now controls your emotions. It controls your decisions. It elevates the pleasure of fulfilled desire above the pleasure of being with God.

Another important truth is this: God would never create desire to be demanding. Urgent, yes, important, yes, but not demanding. Need, when demanding, can lead to fear and loss of faith. However, desire, when demanding, leads to an idol in a person's life that is exalted above God Himself. This is why God often won't allow prayer to be answered if it's coming from an unhealthy perspective regarding desire. When desire masquerades as a need, we put unnatural importance on the fulfillment of that desire. God wants desires to come to pass, but only if we don't need them to!

Here's where so many Christians' issues begin. They have little faith, so needs are often not met and desires demand attention that steals the glory from God.   So these desires then become unholy and unsatisfying.

There is a powerful truth here. Pray in such a way to agree with God, to push back the enemy, to get excited about God's desires for advance, for health, for prosperity, for holy pleasure, for ministry; and then end the prayer with smiling and rejoicing and laughter and freedom!

We are free prior to desire being fulfilled! Our needs have already been met! Our joy comes from the presence of God!

> Psalms 36:8-9 (NIV) They feast on the abundance of your house; you give them drink from your river of delights. For with you is the fountain of life; in your light we see light.

> "Come, all you who are thirsty, come to the waters; and you who have no money, come, buy and eat! Come, buy wine and milk without money and without cost. Why spend money on what is not bread, and your labor on what does not satisfy? Listen, listen to me, and eat what is good, and your soul will delight in the richest of fare. Isaiah 55:1-2 (NIV)

> Then Jesus declared, "I am the bread of life. He who comes to me will never go hungry, and he who believes in me will never be thirsty. John 6:35 (NIV)

> Delight yourself in the LORD and he will give you the desires of your heart. Psalms 37:4 (NIV)

This is why it's so important to be with God. On our own, the enemy can birth illegitimate desires. From the very beginning they will feel like need. There will be no joy in it. We will miss out terribly on focusing on what God wants us to dream about!

So many live their whole lives chasing illegitimate desires that are wearing the mask of need and end up being frustrated, controlling and irritable. They miss the only dreams and desires that God knows will satisfy.

Let's allow God to change us, change our thinking. Let's learn how to believe him, how to dream, how to rejoice.

> I beg you that when I come I may not have to be as bold as I expect to be toward some people who think that we live by the standards of this world. For though we live in the world, we do not wage war as the world does. The weapons we fight with are not the weapons of the world. On the contrary, they have divine power to demolish strongholds. We demolish arguments and every pretension that sets itself up against the knowledge of God, and we take captive every thought to make it obedient to Christ. 2 Corinthians 10:2-5 (NIV)

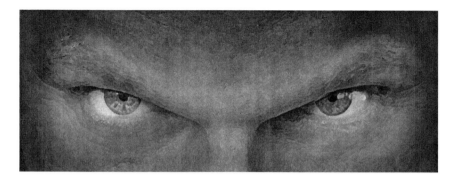

ENEMY NUMBER THREE
HUMAN DESIRE

The previous chapter dealt extensively with the importance of properly identifying what is a need and what is not. Some time was spent on the topic of desire, yet such a powerful world-changing force demands a closer look. We're going to do that now.

There is little complexity to this topic. To deal appropriately with the enemy of human desire, we simply have to discover a way to become invigorated and driven by God-birthed desire.

In all of my years I have not found another way to do this than lengthy, intentional and often difficult prayer. Simply, we must discover God and have the knowledge of God supernaturally imparted into the deepest parts of our being. As this happens, we become alive to what God desires. We don't simply attempt to agree with the Bible, but rather the living Word really and literally burns in us. Revelation awakens us. Our passions and what propels us gets its origins in the very person of the Creator of the world. His designs, His creative power, His dreams–dreams much like those that resulted in galaxies and atoms and you and me coming into being– are revealed to us! Desires that come from that realm are indescribable! And God is yearning to show us these unsearchable realities!

> But if from there you seek the LORD your God, you will find him if you look for him with all your heart and with all your soul. Deuteronomy 4:29 (NIV)
>
> Then you will call upon Me and go and pray to Me, and I will listen to you. And you will seek Me and find Me, when you search for Me with all your heart. Jeremiah 29:12-13 (NKJV)
>
> You shall love the Lord your God with all your heart, with all your soul, and with all your strength. Deuteronomy 6:5 (NKJV)
>
> Then one of them, a lawyer, asked Him a question, testing Him, and saying, "Teacher, which is the great commandment in the law?" Jesus said to him, "'You shall love the Lord your God with all your heart, with all your soul, and with all your mind.' This is the first and great commandment. And the second is like it: 'You shall love your neighbor as yourself.' On these two commandments hang all the Law and the Prophets." Matthew 22:35-40 (NKJV)

There are two specific calls in the above Scriptures (and there are many more such Scriptures in the Bible):

1. The call to seek
2. The call to love

Many Christians find it easier to enjoy what human desire delivers than to enjoy God Himself. Several years ago as I was in bed trying to fall

> Make it easy to enjoy God.

asleep, God spoke what is probably to date the quickest word I've ever received. He said, "Make it easy to enjoy God."

In less than a tenth of a second that message seared my heart. God loves to be enjoyed. He is wooing his Church into a deep and lively encounter with Him. I believe that we should be full of supernaturally charged joy. We should laugh and smile a lot. This is the call for every believer!

So, why is this reality so evasive for so many people? Human desire must be bridled while desire for God must be pursued. Human desire is easy. Nurturing desire for God takes a lot and costs a lot.

> And the Spirit and the bride say, "Come!" And let him who hears say, "Come!" And let him who thirsts come. Whoever desires, let him take the water of life freely. Revelation 22:17 (NKJV)

The call from Jesus to "Come!" resounds night and day. The emerging global ministry of night and day prayer is a response to that call. As we step out in faith and discipline to pursue the living God, as we seek Him with our whole heart, we will find Him. It's not enough to simply want God as we press through our busy schedule every day. We have a duty to take dominion over our calendars and demands of life. To seek is not enough. Many have sought God and haven't found Him. A whole–heart, whole–schedule, whole–energy, whole–focus pursuit of God night and day will result in discovery that will keep us in His presence.

This pursuit in itself will do much more than act as a vehicle from Point A to Point B. As we embrace a fasted lifestyle by eliminating or at least tempering the desires that have ruled our days in the past, we'll find ourselves in a dry place void of satisfaction. Many arrive at the dry place and quit. They turn back to what's familiar and what's an easy fix.

It's in this dry place where our hunger is stirred and our character and integrity come to the surface. Do we really want God or do we want to fulfill shallow desire alone? If we can break through the dry place with passionate seeking for as long as it takes, we will press right into an overwhelming enjoyable encounter with Jesus.

In the dry place we will more easily be able to answer questions of motive. What drives us? What have we been giving ourselves to? What human dreams have consumed our energy?

> Therefore, from now on, we regard no one according to the flesh. Even though we have known Christ according to the flesh, yet now we know Him thus no longer. Therefore, if anyone is in Christ, he is a new creation; old things have passed away; behold, all things have become new. Now all things are of God, who has reconciled us to Himself through Jesus Christ, and has given us the ministry of reconciliation, that is, that God was in Christ reconciling the world to Himself, not imputing their trespasses to them, and has committed to us the word of reconciliation. Now then, we are ambassadors for Christ, as though God were pleading through us: we implore you on Christ's behalf, be reconciled to God. 2 Corinthians 5:16-20 (NKJV)

As we grow in Christ we move away from the old ways of life. Our thought processes, schedules, activities, dreams, pursuits, etc., all change– usually radically. Part of the process of this change is an intentional reconciliation with God. To be reconciled means to be in complete agreement with. The process of complete agreement is progressive, and must be intentional. It takes a person of great passion and determination to press through the draw of the old life into the invisible yet promised abundant life of Jesus.

The last part of that passage says, "Now then, we are ambassadors for Christ, as though God were pleading through us: we implore you on Christ's behalf, be reconciled to God."

That's amazing! This passage speaks volumes to us. To be reconciled doesn't happen naturally, nor is it guaranteed to happen at all. It takes every part of our devotion to accomplish.

Now, I mentioned two specific calls:

1. The call to seek
2. The call to love

Let's talk about the call to love. Have you ever considered this mandate? It's very, very intriguing. I can understand calling someone to serve, to give money, to feed the poor or to avoid sin. That makes sense very easily. However, a mandate to love?

Certainly the act of love in many ways is fully intentional and can often be void of feeling. We act in love toward others. This is also quite easy to understand. But this idea goes well beyond a call to act out in right ways. It's a call to intimacy, a mandate to be deeply intimate with our Lover.

> You shall <u>love</u> the Lord your God with all your heart, with all your soul, and with all your strength. Deuteronomy 6:5 (NKJV)

In the original Hebrew, the word love is ahab.

It means: to have affection for, sexually or otherwise.

Additionally it means to like as a friend.

I don't know about you, but I'm not sure I can be forced to like anybody, much less have deep affection for them. But this is what Scripture is telling us. Could it mean that the call isn't for instant intimacy, but rather a determined and unwavering process of pursuit and faith toward the promise of experiencing an enjoyable God?

As we, in faith, more easily believe that being with God in a continual and significant way will result in continual and significant enjoyment, we will allow the old things to pass away. We will not stop until we discover the joy that only God can provide.

So, if we are to understand that God is mandating us to fall deeply in love with Him, there is a disciplined process that must commence. The goal is deep and passionate intimacy with our Lover, the invisible God.

It makes sense that when we discover this ultimate of pleasures, that we will not be as inclined to pursue the human desires that demanded so much of us in years past. It's been said more times and in more ways than we know, "Our sin causes separation from God. We, in effect, trade intimacy with God for intimacy with the world."

Certainly there is truth to that statement. However, if we view the issue from the other side, we could say, "Intentional pursuit of intimacy with God carries with it the reward of

> Intentional pursuit of intimacy with God carries with it the reward of perpetual discovery.

perpetual discovery. Deliberate surrender of human desire coupled with a craving for the manifest presence of God Himself in our lives will lead, sooner or later, to fulfillment that cannot be measured or effectively explained. It's that extreme. It's that good."

> "You have heard that it was said, 'You shall love your neighbor and hate your enemy.' But I say to you, love your enemies, bless those who curse you, do good to those who hate you, and pray for those who spitefully use you and persecute you … Matthew 5:43-44 (NKJV)

In the above passage, the Hebrew interpretation of the word "love" is different than ahab. It is agapaō, which emphasizes the attitude of love. It's the moral and socially appropriate act of service and attention to others, including both mankind and God Himself.

Throughout Scripture we do see various translations of that single word "love", and God is the central figure regardless of the interpretation. However, it's that unique call to ahab love that has captured my attention. It's a mandate to intimacy.

> I charge you, O daughters of Jerusalem, If you find my beloved, That you tell him I am lovesick! Song of Songs 5:8 (NKJV)

Lovesick! What a word that is. As you might guess, the Hebrew translation is ahab. In the Song of Songs we see this amazing story of love unfold beautifully. In the following verses the word "love" is translated ahab each time. As we gain insight into the intimate longing of our God for us, our hearts melt and our understanding changes.

> "I will rise now," I said, "And go about the city; In the streets and in the squares I will seek the one I love." I sought him, but I did not find him. The watchmen who go about the city found me; I said, "Have you seen the one I love?" Song of Songs 3:2-3 (NKJV)

> [The Shulamite to the Daughters of Jerusalem] He brought me to the banqueting house, And his banner over me was love. Sustain me with cakes of raisins, Refresh me with apples, For I am lovesick. His left hand is under my head, And his right hand embraces me. I charge you, O daughters of Jerusalem, By the gazelles or by the does of the field, Do not stir up nor awaken love Until it pleases. Song of Songs 2:4-7 (NKJV)

> He made its pillars of silver, Its support of gold, Its seat of purple, Its interior paved with love By the daughters of Jerusalem. Song of Songs 3:10 (NKJV)

> How fair and how pleasant you are, O love, with your delights! Song of Songs 7:6 (NKJV)

> [The Shulamite to Her Beloved] Set me as a seal upon your

heart, As a seal upon your arm; For love is as strong as death, Jealousy as cruel as the grave; Its flames are flames of fire, A most vehement flame. Many waters cannot quench love, Nor can the floods drown it. If a man would give for love All the wealth of his house, It would be utterly despised. Song of Songs 8:6-7 (NKJV)

Read the last passage, Song of Songs 8:6-7, over and over. Its communication of passionate desire is intense. As we establish a vow with our Lover, the intentional and disciplined pursuit of intimacy with Him is alluring and strong. It is a vehement flame that even water, the fierce enemy of fire, cannot drown. It's this that we are pursuing, the fire of passion that will overcome the waters of human desire.

In the following Song of Songs passage, we discover a different translation of love.

Draw me away!

[The Daughters of Jerusalem] We will run after you.

[The Shulamite] The king has brought me into his chambers.

[The Daughters of Jerusalem] We will be glad and rejoice in you. We will remember your love more than wine.

[The Shulamite] Rightly do they love you. Song of Songs 1:4 (NKJV)

The Hebrew word used for "love" in the part of the passage that says, "We will remember your love more than wine" is dôd. The literal meaning is to boil. The idea is that God's love is actively boiling. It's hot and constant and intentionally set on us.

The enemy of human desire is a very strong one. A simple resolution to avoid sin and do good is far too weak to be seriously considered for inclusion in our arsenal. The burning fire of passion for God, ahab love, is our most effective weapon. The reward of the perpetual discovery of new depths of God's zeal for us is enough to keep us burning with a vehement flame that the waters of human desire cannot put out.

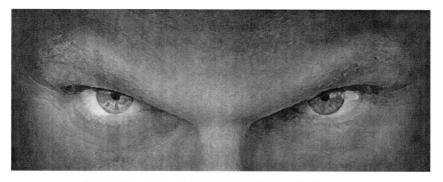

ENEMY NUMBER FOUR
GENERIC DREAMS

From my book, Revelation Driven Prayer:

> If we have a blueprint of the Sears Tower and we put all of our resources into following those blueprints, what will we end up with? Another tower that looks just like the Sears Tower. How strange it would be to see a replica of that building in downtown Denver! Not only would it look silly; it would be a monument to foolishness. To use millions of dollars, thousands upon thousands of man–hours and every ounce of energy over many years to produce a replica of another man's creation is a terrible waste of God's creative resources.

A single question possesses the ability to elicit diametrically opposing emotions and responses when asked of Christians. The question: "What is your vision?"

Some will instantly become invigorated. Their eyes will light up and their previously stoic demeanor suddenly transforms into one of excited joy. As if they had the vision seared into their heart (which is true), they, without hesitance or confusion, breathe the fire of the vision that God burnt into them in years past.

Others, when asked the exact same question, stumble around as their eyes dart around the room, giving them time to think. Frustration is brought to the surface. They don't know. Nothing clear and powerful has been revealed to them.

Many, especially those with responsibilities of leadership such as pastors and church leaders, are left with little option but to look for the latest and greatest visionary idea. Conferences and seminars become the last straw for many of them as they hope, one more time, to discover a workable vision and strategy for their own life and ministry.

The argument would be made that it is wisdom to glean insight from others so our own personal missions are more easily achieved. This is a good argument. It's entirely valid. We should be quick to learn from others' victories and errors. However, this is not a discussion of nuts and bolts but rather of fresh new concepts.

To build a duplicate of the Sears Tower is senseless, though many who have yet to receive the blueprints for their own personal God-given vision have little recourse but to mimic another's. As we allow God to burn into us his plans for the next great structure, the next big dream, we'll use nuts and bolts of old to support and piece together something the world has not yet seen. From my book, *Revelation Driven Prayer:*

Ask ten people what they think some of the non–negotiable elements are for any particular growth strategy and you will get at least 6 different answers. You will also discover some experts, both actual and self-proclaimed, who will be adamant about how you must proceed. Some will have your best interest at heart while others are simply zealous about their past successes, their strategies and their insight. Be humble... and beware!

> Be humble. God will use many different types of people to speak into your life.
> Beware. So will the devil.

If you are truly a person of uncommon sense, you will irritate many who just can't imagine why you can't see things their way. After all, the high majority would side with them! Plus, they have practical experience– their advice is the direct result of what has worked for them and possibly even countless others. They would say that it is tried and true strategy.

The problem? That advice, that strategy that is so obviously effective and appropriate, may simply not be God's desired plan of action for you.

This is a very difficult place for some people to navigate through. A Spirit-driven person with a unique directive from God will not always be able to intellectually explain why he is doing what he is doing. People will believe you are nonsensical when in reality you are simply using a different set of senses. The intellect is taking a backseat to our spirit.

When people come to me with directives and wisdom that is contrary to what God has spoken to me, I will first consider their insight. I will pray about it, sometimes on the spot and sometimes over several days. When the time comes that

I feel led to continue as I have felt the Lord has directed, I'll sometimes challenge the individual, especially if they persist.

I'll ask them to share their understanding of how they feel I should proceed. I'll then alert them to the Scripture that warns us about leaning on our own understanding. We simply cannot assume we know the course another individual should take at all times. We cannot always rely on common sense. In fact, as a believer, MOST of what we do will defy common sense! We should be wary of steps that have been repeated through the ages. We should expect something fresh and new!

We need to know exactly what our specialized calling is. What is it that nobody else on earth has a responsibility to fulfill? What geography, what specialty, what people are we assigned to?

Really, we need to ask the age–old question, "Why am I here?" Certainly there are a variety of answers that are both diverse and valid. Many of the answers would be shared with every other Christian on planet Earth. For example, we are here to be lights in a dark world. The Bible reveals to us that we are to love one another. It's important that each of us does the work of an evangelist. Also, there is a call for all to be saved.

"Look to Me, and be saved, All you ends of the earth! For I am God, and there is no other. Isaiah 45:22 (NKJV)

We could easily fill up the rest of the pages of this book by reviewing the variety of Biblical mandates and callings that are common to all.

That, however, is not what we are discussing here. The question is, "What is your unique calling that was birthed in Heaven and delivered to you alone upon conception in your mother's womb?"

Now, that's a question! As we gain insight into our specialized mission in life, we'll become invigorated and passionate people.

It most certainly requires an intentional departure from our own dreams so we can experience the revelation of God's divine dreams for us.

> Turn away my eyes from looking at worthless things, And revive me in Your way. Psalms 119:37 (NKJV)

Another translation calls for us to turn our eyes from vanity. The sense here is the pursuit of vanity is a pursuit of something that is useless and deceptive. Another way the second part of that verse can be translated is, "revive me in Your journey." I really like this, as the word "journey" communicates purpose and destiny. Or, destination. The idea is that as we look away from distracting things and become revived, we will move ahead on the unique journey God has appointed us to.

In Romans 8 we see a familiar passage of Scripture:

> But if we hope for what we do not see, we eagerly wait for it with perseverance. Likewise the Spirit also helps in our weaknesses. For we do not know what we should pray for as we ought, but the Spirit Himself makes intercession for us with groanings which cannot be uttered. Now He who searches the hearts knows what the mind of the Spirit is, because He makes intercession for the saints according to

the will of God. And we know that all things work together for good to those who love God, to those who are the called according to His purpose. Romans 8:25-28 (NKJV)

The discovery of our mission, mandate and calling will come as we avail ourselves to the working of the Holy Spirit. This passage in Romans certainly speaks to our justification though it also applies to the unveiling of our personal calling.

As we are not only yielded to the Holy Spirit, but also in a place of deep and fervent prayer, the will of God will unfold before us. In Romans 8 we read about the Spirit making intercession for us according to the will of God. This is powerful!

Praying in the Holy Spirit is a critical activity for any of us who are pursuing revelation as to our personal calling in life. That calling will be well beyond what our own personalities, insights, experiences, thoughts, ideas, dreams or passions would point us toward. The revelation of the heart and plans of God will be stirred through groanings and Holy Spirit–driven intercession. As we develop a life of intentional and persistent Holy Spirit driven prayer,

> **Praying in the Holy Spirit is a critical activity for any of us who are pursuing revelation...**

we'll find the pure, precise will of God come to light. Intercession that is initiated and carried by God Himself will be overwhelmingly effective.

Without the revelation of God's humanly impossible dreams that are birthed and revealed in the invisible realm of intercession, we will find ourselves defaulting to what our own minds and imaginations can invent. We'll look for the latest and greatest strategy and try to imitate it. If we do this, we will have no choice but to ask God to bless our human plans instead of us blessing God's divine plans.

So, the question now presents itself, where do I start?

1. Continual Prayer

    This topic is addressed from a variety of perspectives throughout this book. Suffice it to say that we simply have no option but to become people of lengthy, continual prayer. Praying in tongues, as mentioned just previously, is a critical piece of the puzzle of discovery. It's in this place of deep pursuit into the center of God's heart where we will begin to see with new eyes. Revelation will suddenly emerge and we'll find ourselves coming alive in dynamic new ways.

    "Ask, and it will be given to you; seek, and you will find; knock, and it will be opened to you. For everyone who asks receives, and he who seeks finds, and to him who knocks it will be opened. Matthew 7:7-8 (NKJV)

    I like looking at this passage as a progression into the place of revelation. Oftentimes we can find ourselves stopping after asking God for what He wants to give us. From cover to cover in Scripture we know that God has promised many things to His children. As we ask, it's a simple step of faith; and according to this particular passage of Scripture, we see that upon asking God does give it to us. His promises are "Yes" and "Amen"!

However, though God has given us things, including our destiny and callings, there is much more for us to do before we actually possess them.

The life of continual prayer will compel us to not only ask, but to seek! From time to time my boys and I will go geocaching. If you have never done this, I highly recommend you try it out at least once. It's adventurous family fun!

First, you need to buy or borrow a GPS unit. Then, you go to a special web site and type in the zip code of where you would like your adventure to take place. You then enter your preferences such as difficulty of the terrain, whether you want to walk on trails, in an urban area or through the woods, etc. The site will return to you a variety of geocaching journeys for you to embark on.

The site also gives you the most important detail: the exact GPS longitude and latitude. Before you start the journey, you need the coordinates. At this point the excitement really starts to ramp up! There will be some sort of treasure in a place you've never been, and it's worth the time, energy and effort to get there. The journey is half the fun!

So, we could say that the interaction with the web site is the 'asking' part of the journey. We enter our request, and we receive a guarantee of an adventure and a prize.

I press toward the goal for the prize of the upward call of God in Christ Jesus. Philippians 3:14 (NKJV)

Now, we begin seeking! We'll get in the car with the GPS and drive as close as we can to the hidden treasure. We then park and head off into new territory! We must stay focused, watching the coordinates on the GPS change with every step, in order to ensure we reach our goal.

So it was, after three days, that the officers went through the camp; and they commanded the people, saying, "When you see the ark of the covenant of the Lord your God, and the priests, the Levites, bearing it, then you shall set out from your place and go after it. Yet there shall be a space between you and it, about two thousand cubits by measure. Do not come near it, that you may know the way by which you must go, for you have not passed this way before." Joshua 3:2-4 (NKJV)

We've never been this way before! As we are in a place of continual prayer, we will discover more and more how to hear His voice, to see Him move and to follow His lead. I remember when I first went geocaching, how it took some time to figure out how to read it. On my particular unit there was some translation that was necessary, and I didn't realize this. So, the boys and I went walking in huge circles around a wooded neighborhood. I'll never forget the moment that "I got it!" I figured out how to read the GPS accurately. I made a bee line down a trail right to the general location where the treasure was supposed to be buried. The adrenaline was surging!

A container with the above lable was hiding somewhere very close to where I was standing! After many circles and aimless wanderings I was finally there! There were bushes and trees and large rocks in the small area where the GPS led me. The boys and I looked everywhere. We were seeking with passion! Suddenly, as I was walking through some low bushes, I felt something under my foot. I looked down and there it was! I called the kids over and they were jumping up and down. After an amazing adventure we found the prize! The prize that we knew was there all along. It was promised to us when we searched for it on the web site. Everything we needed for the journey was given to us, even though we had to take some time to learn the process by walking in circles and discovering how to read and translate the GPS.

This whole procedure in our spiritual lives is best described as "walking in the Spirit." We move out in faith and continually check the coordinates as we move forward.

Now it was time to knock on that container! It was opened and inside were some trinkets and a journal to record our discovery. We took a toy and left a toy and signed the journal for the next person to read. We closed it up and buried it again. Our journey for the day was over, and it was back to the web site to find our coordinates for our next mission!

Simply put, we ask, then start the faith–filled journey of seeking and then knock and watch the treasures of God open up to us! This is the first step in discovering our God-given callings: continual prayer.

2. Serve another person as he pursues his destiny

My hope is that you will easily notice that the pursuit of a fulfilled destiny isn't an overnight process. The first step, continual prayer, is what launches us but it's also what sustains us. That phase will never end. So, in the midst of your journey of continual prayer, of asking, seeking and knocking, you should ask God what leaders you should watch and serve.

This step is, in my opinion, non–negotiable. From cover to cover in the Word of God we see this pattern unfold. God's chosen leaders found themselves in an often lengthy position of serving another leader. It's in this place of submission to another where we will discover volumes about our character, the condition of our heart, improper ambition (as opposed to proper and godly ambition), pride, insecurities and other personal issues that have the potential of nullifying our future missions.

It is not good to have zeal without knowledge, nor to be hasty and miss the way. Proverbs 19:2 (NIV)

In my short time in ministry here on the planet, I've sadly witnessed many zealous and wonderful people miss the way because of their lack of knowledge. Instead of having a servant's heart, so often their zeal gets the best of them and causes them to become frustrated and often critical toward those whom God has placed in their lives to sharpen them. God will allow us to endure years of hiddenness and being irritated and pressed in situations that stretch us to our very limits. If we lose sight of the fact that God is allowing our zeal to be tempered in the school of wisdom and knowledge, we will find ourselves wandering and complaining for decades.

But if we realize that our ultimate knocking and the resulting opening of God's destiny for us may not fully activate until we're 70 or 80 years of age, then we'll settle in for the long haul and allow the process of refining to continue. Of course, something may initiate much sooner than that, but do your best to remember the excitement of the journey. Serve well, learn much and get ready for what's coming. Just possibly, the greater the calling, the greater the schooling that will be necessary.

I have heard it said that here in America it's common to attend a ministry school or college for two to four years and then embark on thirty–plus years of ministry. However, Jesus prepared for his ministry for thirty years for three years of ministry. Is it possible that God has us on a thirty– or forty–year track of serving and gleaning wisdom and knowledge so we can minister with maturity for a few years near the end of our lives? Regardless of the exact process, the truth is that much education in the school of life as we serve others with excellence will result in much maturity, insight, strength and wisdom if we press on with integrity and a humble heart.

> Let us not become weary in doing good, for at the proper time we will reap a harvest if we do not give up. Galatians 6:9 (NIV)

The KJV tells us that we will reap if we "faint not." There is a lot of fainting in the church! As we understand that there may be years between the time of asking and opening we will be careful to "faint not" and persevere.

A couple of years ago I was in one of the prophecy rooms at the International House of Prayer in Kansas City, Missouri. I received some amazingly accurate prophetic words on this particular day, as I had in the past. I stood up to leave when one of the people in the room said, "I have one more question for you that I believe God would want you to consider." He had my attention. This person knew nothing about me or my ministry. In fact, he didn't know that I was in ministry at all.

He said, "God wants to ask you a question. If it takes another twenty years before your ministry is fulfilled, before the  vision is finally seen, will you still contend?"

The secret blessing that I received in that moment was my surprising reaction at the deepest core of my heart. Ten years ago this word would have frustrated me considerably. However on this day I felt the life of God burning deep within as my instant reaction to this question was, "Of course. What else would I do?"

I was wonderfully surprised. God set me up in such a way that I was powerfully encouraged even though the journey was far from over. In fact, the blessing is discovered bit by bit on the journey, not only at the place of final fulfillment.

So, how do we spend our time on the journey? Much of it will be spent being sharpened and trained by other men and women. God will use those who are greatly gifted and those who are not, those who are mature and those who are not. The call is not for us to only find the greatest leaders in the nation to grow from, but also to allow God to place us under some who are weaker. Their weakness will do wonders in testing our own humility as we submit to and serve them well.

David came to Saul and entered his service. Saul liked him very much, and David became one of his armor-bearers. 1 Samuel 16:21 (NIV)

3. Let your dream die

As with the previous point, the process of allowing your dream to die may very well begin almost any time. A very effective test of one's character is the test of dead dreams. This idea was touched on during our discussion about serving another person's dream, but it's such an important step that it warrants its own discussion.

A personal call of God is so, well, deeply personal that it can get the best of us. Simply the call and mandate can demand our affection even beyond what we would give God Himself. God is very aware of the power of a calling, a dream and a vision. He designed it this way. But, we know all too well that God is jealous and will not allow anything, including God-breathed vision, to receive worship.

We must be very careful not to allow our vision to be the source of our identity. If it is, we will fight at all cost against anything that might threaten the advance of that vision– even God.

It's so easy to become discouraged and to feel rejected if we aren't released to run with our vision. Many will go from church to church looking for an environment where they can be free to function within their calling, all while God is actually calling them to let the calling die!

Any pastor who has been through some trials (that would be any of them who have been in pastoral ministry more than a month!) would admit that they proceed with great caution when disgruntled people decide to call their church home. The red flags start to wave furiously when someone says something like, "My last church was good, but I just didn't feel free to minister according to my calling there."

A critical question at this point must be asked of the new arrival, "Have you ever let that calling die?"

If not, a continual season of frustration awaits that individual. How often do we find ourselves with a precious and promising seed in our hands only to wonder why it's not growing and developing? The object lesson is obvious yet powerful. We have absolutely no ability to cause a seed to grow. It must be released into the soil of brokenness, prayer and humility. Only then, according to God's timing and not ours, will the seed eventually transform into what it's called to be. Just as with a seed, the most fragile and critical phase of growth comes in the early stages of hiddenness and trial.

I know a pastor who won't allow anybody in the church to function in a leadership role until they have been there for two years. This is to err on the side of wisdom. Those who want to function in their calling because their identity is found there won't last in a church like that. However, those that are simply there to serve will thrive, and it will be obvious to all.

We really need to trust God in this entire process. Something I truly love to do is teach and preach. I find myself invigorated when I am able to do so. However, I do my best to surrender that desire and gifting to God by understanding that, while I personally enjoy teaching, God may not need my teaching in the season I'm in. Simply, if God needs me to teach, He'll open the door and I'll teach. If He doesn't need me to teach, I won't teach.

We should lay every calling, dream, vision, gifting, talent and desire on the altar continually. If God needs us to die, be broken, learn, mature, serve, surrender and grow from a place of hiddenness deep in the soil of His nourishment, we may not be called on to teach, lead a small group, start a church, pastor, be an elder or run ahead in any other ministry for a season. This season is non–negotiable if we are to be effective for decades and decades.

Of course, we know we are to 'die daily,' so the process of death will be continual, as will the resulting process of life. So, this critical point will be both perpetual in one sense and seasonal in another sense. We die every day and we die for entire seasons, many times throughout our lives.

4. Humbly and boldly take a risk.

A generic dream takes you where many have been before. A dream imparted personally into the depths of your inner man from God Himself requires that you go where no man has gone before. To live this way requires faith. Huge faith.

> A generic dream takes you where many have been before.

I'll never forget the moment God called me to transition Revolution Church into Revolution House of Prayer. The mandate was clear and the long process of preparation in my own life was culminating in a moment of decision on the carpet at the altar at the front of the sanctuary. I was all alone. It was just God, me, and a call to risk everything. I had to respond.

I told God three things as I sat there in that empty room:

> First, I told God that if I responded to the call to be a furnace of prayer as a primary, foundational function of our ministry, many people would leave. God didn't respond.

> Second, I told God that we'd lose money. My salary, our house payment, vacations, everything was at risk. God said nothing.

> Third, as I sat there feeling both alone and comforted at the same time, I mentioned to God

that, if we made this move, I'd lose my reputation.
God finally spoke. He said, "Good."

You see, God's Son was of no reputation. Why should I hold tight to my own? So we took the plunge and everything we risked, we did lose, at least to a degree. It was probably the hardest thing my family has ever gone through, yet I cringe at the thought of not making that crucial decision that day. I could still be the senior pastor of Revolution Church, and we'd still have some good services and some good ministries. However, my destiny and the destiny of Manitou Springs would have been sacrificed. No revival. No transformation.

It's in the season of risk, faith and pressing toward the goal that the purposes of the other steps of continual prayer, serving another's vision and allowing our own God–given dream to die become radically evident. You see, those phases never end. We will have to pray always, serve others with fervor and die daily if we are to survive the season of risky advance. To try to move ahead in our callings without having gone through those basic yet deeply reforming seasons would result in short–lived success at best and utter failure and great damage to our families and other precious people at worst.

To conclude this discussion of generic dreams versus God–birthed dreams, visions, callings and mandates, suffice it to say this: You will find great joy and life, as will many others, as you press through a variety of important difficult phases into the fire-refined seasons of precise and personal mission advance.

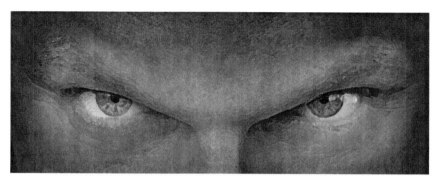

ENEMY NUMBER FIVE
A BELIEF IN FATE

Let's begin this discussion on fate by bringing some correction to a word in the title of this book. I purposely used the word "destiny" for a couple of reasons, even though it's not the best word when discussing a believer's calling.

First, the idea of destiny is something that every person considers. We wonder what the big picture holds. It's an easy concept to understand.

Second, highlighting the dictionary definition of the word destiny will help bring understanding to the enemy we're revealing in this chapter: fate.

Destiny:
- A predetermined course of events considered as something beyond human power or control
- An event (or a course of events) that will inevitably happen in the future

Now let's look at the definition of the word "fate".

Fate:
- Something that unavoidably befalls a person; fortune; lot
- That which is inevitably predetermined; destiny

So, destiny and fate have a lot in common. It's very important to understand that much of what God has called us into will not occur without our radical participation.

We need to know that we must hear God, receive His Word, understand it and obey it in order for our destiny or calling to be fulfilled. We are to be vigilant participants in this grand mission of God.

Let's look at a fairly long passage of Scripture. I encourage you to read through it in its entirety, even though I'm confident you may know the story quite well:

> And Jesus answered and spoke to them again by parables and said: "The kingdom of heaven is like a certain king who arranged a marriage for his son, and sent out his servants to call those who were invited to the wedding; and they were not willing to come. Again, he sent out other servants, saying, 'Tell those who are invited, "See, I have prepared my dinner; my oxen and fatted cattle are killed, and all things are ready. Come to the wedding."' But they made light of it and went their ways, one to his own farm, another to his business. And the rest seized his servants, treated them spitefully, and killed them. But when the king heard about it, he was furious. And he sent out his armies, destroyed those murderers, and burned up their city. Then he said to his servants, 'The wedding is ready, but those who were invited

were not worthy. Therefore go into the highways, and as many as you find, invite to the wedding.' So those servants went out into the highways and gathered together all whom they found, both bad and good. And the wedding hall was filled with guests. But when the king came in to see the guests, he saw a man there who did not have on a wedding garment. So he said to him, 'Friend, how did you come in here without a wedding garment?' And he was speechless. Then the king said to the servants, 'Bind him hand and foot, take him away, and cast him into outer darkness; there will be weeping and gnashing of teeth.' For many are called, but few are chosen." Matthew 22:1-14 (NKJV)

Many are called, but few are chosen. This powerful account makes it quite clear that while God has made preparation, we must respond. We are to be diligently responsive and ready when the call of God is sounded. To

> This enemy of fulfilled destiny is the embracing of destiny itself.

be called is not to be chosen! We cannot ever assume that our calling will somehow just develop without our participation. This enemy of fulfilled destiny is the embracing of destiny itself.

Let's look at another Scripture that gives further revelation on this topic:

These will make war with the Lamb, and the Lamb will overcome them, for He is Lord of lords and King of kings; and those who are with Him are called, chosen, and faithful." Revelation 17:14 (NKJV)

It's clear that we must not only be called, but also chosen. And, further, we must be faithful. It's an entirely interactive, participatory and immersive life that we are to live.

> "Go, assemble the elders of Israel and say to them, 'The LORD, the God of your fathers--the God of Abraham, Isaac and Jacob-- appeared to me and said: I have watched over you and have seen what has been done to you in Egypt. And I have promised to bring you up out of your misery in Egypt into the land of the Canaanites, Hittites, Amorites, Perizzites, Hivites and Jebusites--a land flowing with milk and honey.'" Exodus 3:16-17 (NIV)

This is only one of many passages of Scripture that reveal God's promise to give a new land to His people. Of course, we know the story: The promise was never realized by an entire generation! Even Moses himself didn't enter Caanan.

> "Behold, I stand at the door and knock. If anyone hears My voice and opens the door, I will come in to him and dine with him, and he with Me. "To him who overcomes I will grant to sit with Me on My throne, as I also overcame and sat down with My Father on His throne. "He who has an ear, let him hear what the Spirit says to the churches." Revelation 3:20-22 (NKJV)

Again we see a passage of Scripture that highlights the truth that a successfully fulfilled mission, whether its the mission of salvation, taking cities for Jesus, growing in ministry or enjoying a God-fueled, successful business, is contingent on our agreement with and response to the directives of God.

Now, I understand that this point may seem on the surface to be quite obvious. However, given the national deficiency in the realm of spiritual fervor and both personal and corporate passion, it seems more obvious that there must be a disconnect. There are so many enemies of fulfilled destiny (we can still use that word now that we've changed the definition for the sake of this book!), many more enemies than this book addresses, that we can't give in to one that is so easily defeated.

Though this enemy is such a simple one to conquer (after all, its defeat simply requires us to unlearn wrong ideas and replace them with biblical truths), if not addressed we can find ourselves growing more cynical, discouraged, angry and disillusioned as the years go by. This enemy has phenomenal ability to steal decades and entire lifetimes!

> Be glad then, you children of Zion, And rejoice in the Lord your God; For He has given you the former rain faithfully, And He will cause the rain to come down for you-- The former rain, And the latter rain in the first month. The threshing floors shall be full of wheat, And the vats shall overflow with new wine and oil. "So I will restore to you the years that the swarming locust has eaten, The crawling locust, The consuming locust, And the chewing locust, My great army which I sent among you. Joel 2:23-25 (NKJV)

Man's lack of response to the directives of God have, time and again throughout Scripture, resulted in great loss. In Joel we see our great Redeemer promising restoration. In our human condition we all make mistakes, both small and large. It's a constant prayer in my heart that the years of failure would be redeemed. Scripture makes it very clear that it's quite possible to lose precious years due to disobedience, apathy and wrong ideas in the area of fate.

> Therefore He says: "Awake, you who sleep, Arise from the dead, And Christ will give you light." See then that you walk circumspectly, not as fools but as wise, redeeming the time, because the days are evil. Therefore do not be unwise, but understand what the will of the Lord is. Ephesians 5:14-17 (NKJV)

Wake up! That's the call to the church! When there is an awakening, then the light of Christ comes. Then we are to walk! The verse tells us to walk circumspectly. What does this mean?

> Circumspectly: watchful and discreet; cautious; prudent; well-considered

So as we decide to awaken and walk in a well-considered manner, we will find our time redeemed. Then the key to it all is the call, the mandate, to understand what the will of the Lord is! We simply don't have an option. Why? Because we have a major role in the process. If we don't respond, the mission is in great jeopardy.

This really calls for a sober outlook, a serious demeanor. If we don't make steps to fulfill our destiny, our ministry, then who knows how many lives hang in the balance? The enemy would tell us to relax and don't advance. He'll convince us that we have little or no role to play in the grand scheme of things. He'll say that it'll all work out in the end. The truth is that, no, it won't. Not always. Not usually.

Allow me to share a personal story. Most of my life I have endeavoured to live as righteously as possible. My relationship with

God was precious to me even at an early age. I was blessed to not have to struggle with drugs, foul language and other snares. However, there was a sliver of time in the late 1980s where I found myself failing with alcohol.

It's tragic what a misstep can do, even if it only covers a few days, weeks or months of one's life. I worked as a pizza delivery driver and would often hang out at the store even on my days off. One night I went to a bar with some of the guys from work and had three or four drinks too many. Now, everybody knew of my church history and that I just recently went to Bible college. I shared often about the miracles of God, of healings and the amazing things I had experienced and witnessed.

After we were done at the bar, we all ended up at the pizza store. I'll never forget what happened next. An older man that I worked with who, as far as I knew, was single, lonely and usually quite sad, approached me. I didn't really realize it, but this man would listen to my stories about God and church with great interest. I was sitting on a counter, well under the influence, and I watched as he walked over to me. He hung his head low and then looked up to me. He said one thing with great sadness and hopelessness in his voice, "I thought you were a Christian."

That was it. There was no condemnation or mocking in his voice. It was quite the opposite. It felt as if his last ounce of hope had just disappeared, and it was my fault.

Now, when I share this story, many times some very nice and well–meaning people will tell me, "John, you need to know that you don't have to carry this. You are forgiven."

Yes, I am forgiven. No, I don't live in condemnation. However, I also don't believe in fate. Everything isn't magically all right. To this day, though I've prayed intently for this man over the years, I understand that my failure may be the straw that broke the camel's back. It's easily possible that our failures result in people living in hell for eternity. To dismiss this reality is to abdicate our responsibility. Everything doesn't simply work out okay. If it did, we would never have to pray, missions would be unnecessary, and ministry itself would be pointless.

You see, all around us babies are aborted every day. People are murdered. Others commit suicide. People are full of fear, depression and hatred. Everything is not okay, and everything won't be okay if we believe in fate. We must work hard.

> So teach us to number our days, That we may gain a heart of wisdom. Psalms 90:12 (NKJV)

There were a certain number of my days where my failure caused damage. I can't afford to make that mistake again.

> I charge you therefore before God and the Lord Jesus Christ, who will judge the living and the dead at His appearing and His kingdom: Preach the word! Be ready in season and out of season. Convince, rebuke, exhort, with all longsuffering and teaching. For the time will come when they will not endure sound doctrine, but according to their own desires, because they have itching ears, they will heap up for themselves teachers; and they will turn their ears away from the truth, and be turned aside to fables. But you be watchful in all things, endure afflictions, do the work of an evangelist, fulfill your ministry. 2 Timothy 4:1-5 (NKJV)

Do you notice the alarm that this passage is sounding? The great Judge will respond to the actions of mankind, and the call here is to be ready! The mandate for you and me is to be watchful, to endure and to fulfill. It's up to us as we are empowered by the living God.

The second half of this particular story is a grand display of the redemption of God. While, as I said, I'll never know if the man in the pizza store ever found Jesus, and that truth will hurt forever, I watched God's love for me unfold in a special, personal way one day.

As I said, there was a very short time in the late 1980s when I lived quite poorly. It wasn't long after that when my life caught the fire of God in a dramatic way. I've never been the same again. In early 2001 I was working in a call center as I was planting Revolution Church in Manitou Springs, Colorado. There was a man there that in many ways reminded me of the man in the pizza store. Not in every way, certainly, but there were several attributes that were strikingly similar.

> ...if I ever decided to be a Christian, I'd want to be just like you.

I never talked with this man directly, as he worked in another part of the building, though from time to time we'd pass in the hall. One day, seemingly out of the blue as we were about to pass by each other in the hallway, he stopped me. Just as the man over a decade earlier spoke one short sentence that shook me to the core, this man spoke one short sentence that nearly brought tears to my eyes. He said, "You know what? I've watched you; and if I ever decided to be a Christian, I'd want to be just like you."

Then he simply walked on. My weak devotion to serve Jesus touched a man whom I didn't even know. Was it fate? No. I played a part, however small it was. Our small, weak, imperfect determination to love Jesus may be minute, but it is by no means insignificant. Two men in my life were forever touched by my intentional decisions. I pray for the first. I thank God for the second.

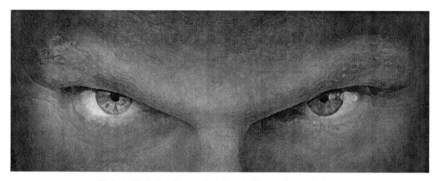

ENEMY NUMBER SIX
RELIANCE ON MAN

Allow me to begin addressing this final enemy by making an important qualifying statement. A foundational component of God's government (His way of delegating and administering) on the Earth is the facilitation of ministry through mankind. God uses people in a variety of very important manners in order for Kingdom life to function well. In this divine and diverse system God has established a system of interdependence. I need you and you need me.

Added to this key truth is the very important principle of submission. We must submit to one another, and we must most certainly submit to our authorities. I address this topic more comprehensively in my book Covens in the Church. We are not called to be anarchists who embrace a non-Biblical methodology of self-governance. God's government demands humble submission to others in our lives.

It's from this position and attitude of service where God can more effectively trust His children to become holy dreamers. God can entrust divine missions to us when He knows that our heart is bent on loving others well and preferring them above ourselves.

The problem comes when healthy interdependence gives way to burdensome co–dependence. All sorts of issues arise when we find ourselves being frustrated and held back in ministry and attaching blame to other people. If we align ourselves with this enemy, we'll be fooled into thinking that the fulfillment of our ministry is fully dependent on our pastor or leader.

Does God use others to help facilitate our ministry? Yes. Are we to take it upon ourselves to determine how others are to facilitate our ministry? No. God has called us to serve. True ministry is actually service. So, as servants, we humbly avail ourselves to others and do our best to help them in their ministry.

> "When you are invited by anyone to a wedding feast, do not sit down in the best place, lest one more honorable than you be invited by him; and he who invited you and him come and say to you, 'Give place to this man,' and then you begin with shame to take the lowest place. But when you are invited, go and sit down in the lowest place, so that when he who invited you comes he may say to you, 'Friend, go up higher.' Then you will have glory in the presence of those who sit at the table with you. For whoever exalts himself will be humbled, and he who humbles himself will be exalted." Luke 14:8-11 (NKJV)

As we truly embrace the principle of preferring others above ourselves, it will actually feel unusual to expect others to make a place for us and our ministry. Instead of becoming frustrated when a place isn't made for us, we'll be at peace knowing that God is fully in charge of our destiny. We can serve well, expect nothing, be fearless of rejection and allow the process of biblical promotion to naturally take place.

When that issue is resolved, you can focus on the journey of personal development and preparation for the ministry that God has called you to. If a call to preach has been burned in your heart, then in due time you will most certainly preach, but not before you are ready. God may use others to create a divine delay in your ministry. Don't blame others for this speed bump. You aren't to be reliant on others, but you are to avail yourself to others. Serve them well.

> For whoever exalts himself will be humbled, and he who humbles himself will be exalted." Luke 14:11 (NKJV)

Your promotion isn't dependent on others noticing your greatness, but rather is on the revelation of your weakness! When humility becomes the driving force in our lives, God gets very excited about the powerful ministry that will eventually flow through us.

> And supper being ended, the devil having already put it into the heart of Judas Iscariot, Simon's son, to betray Him, Jesus, knowing that the Father had given all things into His hands, and that He had come from God and was going to God, rose from supper and laid aside His garments, took a towel and girded Himself. After that, He poured water into a basin and began to wash the disciples' feet, and to wipe them with the towel with which He was girded. John 13:2-5 (NKJV)

Jesus was about to experience mankind enforcing their rule over him. However, no matter how resistant other people were to the ministry of Jesus, God would not be denied! Pontius Pilate couldn't stop the earthshaking ministry of Jesus. Judas couldn't. The guards couldn't. Jesus prevailed.

> No man can stop what God desires to do through our lives as we surrender in complete humility.

This act of humility, as Jesus washed the feet of His disciples, was a visible revelation of the condition of His heart and character. Our call to humility is the same. No man can stop what God desires to do through our lives as we surrender in complete humility.

Our destiny will be facilitated in many ways through God's government on Earth; however no man can stand in the way of our fulfilled destiny. Our reliance is on God, not man.

Often, people will leave churches because their ministry isn't received. It's hindered or even rejected. For example, someone may feel a calling to sing on the worship team. The worship team leadership, however, may not feel that this particular person is a good fit for the team. It can be very easy for the individual to allow offense to take root in their heart. Their thought is that the worship leader is standing in the way of God and is stifling the Holy Spirit. This person can easily embrace a divisive spirit, bitterness and anger. So, in frustration they just leave in hopes of finding a more enlightened leader who will allow them to minister.

This scenario tragically occurs every day in churches around the world. Rebellion to authority is embraced along with a heart of accusation as they take their immaturity to the next church on their unhealthy journey to personal affirmation.

Ministry is service. If a church doesn't need our particular gifting to be expressed, then that's OK. We serve another way. If God needs us to sing, to preach or to work in a particular function He will make sure that no man can stand in our way. Ministry, though personally fulfilling, isn't about personal fulfillment. It's about service.

Check out Paul's description of ministry:

> We put no stumbling block in anyone's path, so that our ministry will not be discredited. Rather, as servants of God we commend ourselves in every way: in great endurance; in troubles, hardships and distresses; in beatings, imprisonments and riots; in hard work, sleepless nights and hunger; in purity, understanding, patience and kindness; in the Holy Spirit and in sincere love; in truthful speech and in the power of God; with weapons of righteousness in the right hand and in the left; through glory and dishonor, bad report and good report; genuine, yet regarded as impostors; known, yet regarded as unknown; dying, and yet we live on; beaten, and yet not killed; sorrowful, yet always rejoicing; poor, yet making many rich; having nothing, and yet possessing everything. 2 Corinthians 6:3-10 (NIV)

Are you sure you want to minister? Though the question is sobering and thought-provoking, the answer for all of us must remain "Yes." We are called to minister, however true ministry as defined in Scripture may be something quite different than many think. It's a call to wash feet and to die at the hands of others. It's a tragic yet precious calling.

We were not looking for praise from men, not from you or anyone else. As apostles of Christ we could have been a burden to you ... 1 Thessalonians 2:6 (NIV)

We are hard pressed on every side, but not crushed; perplexed, but not in despair; persecuted, but not abandoned; struck down, but not destroyed. We always carry around in our body the death of Jesus, so that the life of Jesus may also be revealed in our body. For we who are alive are always being given over to death for Jesus' sake, so that his life may be revealed in our mortal body. So then, death is at work in us, but life is at work in you. 2 Corinthians 4:8-12 (NIV)

If our destiny is to minister (it is!), then we must grab hold of the amazing example of Paul and other biblical leaders. In these two passages alone we discover:

- We are not to seek praise (affirmation, promotion, etc.) from man.
- We are not to be a burden.
- Though hard pressed we are not to be crushed.

Truly, our destiny, as Paul emphasized, is to die. The very people that we wanted our promotion to come through may actually be those that disappoint us and cause our flesh to die. God values the process of killing pride, selfish ambition and other obstacles to pure ministry. We must understand

> The very people that we wanted our promotion to come through may actually be those that disappoint us and cause our flesh to die.

this if we are to come out of this healthy and invigorated! God is calling us to minister with power, and this reality should take us well beyond our own personal fulfillment when we are able to minister according to our own giftings and desires.

Our destiny will not be held back by pastors, leaders, friends, parents or anybody else, but God will use these people to facilitate the process of brokenness that is so necessary in our lives.

As we allow this process to happen, and refuse to indict others, a humble and burning man or woman of God will emerge as a powerful weapon in the hands of the living God!

> Brothers, think of what you were when you were called. Not many of you were wise by human standards; not many were influential; not many were of noble birth. But God chose the foolish things of the world to shame the wise; God chose the weak things of the world to shame the strong. He chose the lowly things of this world and the despised things--and the things that are not--to nullify the things that are, so that no one may boast before him. It is because of him that you are in Christ Jesus, who has become for us wisdom from God--that is, our righteousness, holiness and redemption. Therefore, as it is written: "Let him who boasts boast in the Lord." 1 Corinthians 1:26-31 (NIV)

It's from a humble, vulnerable place where we can allow God to flow through our weaknesses. God receives the glory and we boast in Him alone. It's our reflection of the glory of God that will most quickly result in fulfilled destiny. As we shine Jesus, the world will crave what we have to impart.

As a prisoner for the Lord, then, I urge you to live a life worthy of the calling you have received. Be completely humble and gentle; be patient, bearing with one another in love. Make every effort to keep the unity of the Spirit through the bond of peace. Ephesians 4:1-3 (NIV)

So, the message of humility should be quite obvious at this point. The very simple conclusion for us as we pursue a fulfilled destiny and ministry is this: Rely on God and trust His process. God will use people to both encourage us and discipline us. They will be used to refine us and promote us. They are instruments in God's hands. Don't get upset at the instruments if they don't recognize you. Serve them well and trust God to make you ready for the ministry that He has called you to.

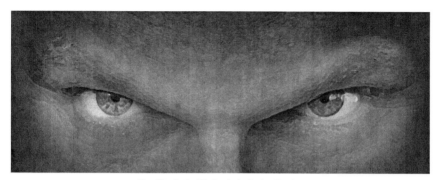

CONCLUSION

My prayer is that you are truly excited about your journey. Fulfilling our destiny, calling and ministry requires much on our part. As we make a firm decision to fight back every enemy with fervency, we'll watch God move in unique ways in our lives.

Don't grow weary in doing good. Stand firm. Be humble. Dream big. Crucify your flesh. Die daily. Pray continually. Press hard. God is very much with you.

> Not that I have already obtained all this, or have already been made perfect, but I press on to take hold of that for which Christ Jesus took hold of me. Brothers, I do not consider myself yet to have taken hold of it. But one thing I do: Forgetting what is behind and straining toward what is ahead, I press on toward the goal to win the prize for which God has called me heavenward in Christ Jesus. Philippians 3:12-14 (NIV)

Other Revival Nation books by John Burton

A book by John's wife, Amy Burton

THE SIGNIFICANT LIFE

During the lonely weeks and months following the death of their unborn or newly born child, most parents seek to affirm the existence of their baby. Well-intentioned comments such as, "It's for the best," or "You can have another one," minimize the significance of the lost child and suggest that he or she was irrelevant or replaceable. The Significant Life seeks to meet the most basic needs of bereaved parents by validating their grief and celebrating the life of their miscarried or stillborn son or daughter. The Significant Life enables parents to confront their emotions and work toward grief resolution. As the author shares her story of personal loss, she guides the reader toward hope and restoration. Every step of this healing journey commemorates a life that, however brief, has left his or her parents eternally changed.

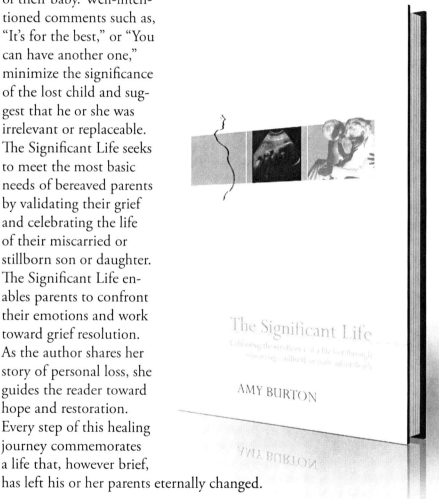

ORDER ONLINE AT WWW.JOHNBURTON.NET

Printed in the United States
151509LV00003B/13/P